There's a Babirusa in My Bathtub!

New Edition

Fact & Fancy About Curious Creatures

By Maxine Rose Schur

Illustrated By Michael S. Maydak

For my adorable great nephews, Josiah and Aleksander — MRS

To Wolf and Teal, may you explore the uniqueness of the world — MSM

Additional Resources
can be found on the
Lawley Publishing Website
Check out:
www.lawleypublishing.com/resources

This edition first published in 2021 by Lawley Publishing, a division of Lawley Enterprises LLC.

Copyright © 2021 by Maxine Rose Schur
All Rights Reserved

Lawley Publishing
70 S. Val Vista Dr. #A3 #188
Gilbert, AZ. 85296
www.LawleyPublishing.com

You've heard of cats
and you've heard of bats
and giraffes
and zebras, of course.
You've heard of birds
and know so many words
for creatures like the
elephant,
fox and horse.

But outside a zoo,
what would you do
with an animal you didn't know?
Do you think you'd be frightened?
Or want to be enlightened?
If so...
turn these pages and go!

Babirusa
(bab-uh-ROO-suh)

Fabulous Fact
To prove who is strongest, male babirusas stand on their hind legs and box each other.

There's a babirusa in my bathtub
I sure wish he'd get out.
I'd fight with him about it
But he's got tusks on his snout.

There's a babirusa in my bathtub
And I wish he'd go away,
But he looks so very fearful
I'm much too scared to say
"GO AWAY!"

He's splashing all the water
And making a big mess.
Yet when he asks me if I like it
I answer **"YES! YES! YES!"**

The babirusa would never leave your bathtub because it loves water. It especially loves to swim long distances. In its great hunt for food, a babirusa will swim from one island to another.

People in Indonesia call the babirusa a pig-deer because it has legs like a deer and a face like a pig. And what a face! The babirusa has the strangest tusks of any animal. The top pair grows upward and curves backwards like horns, sometimes piercing the skin of its face. The lower pair sticks out between the lips and also curves upwards. These four big tusks make the babirusa look more dangerous than it really is.

Babirusas live in groups of about eight. A group of babirusas is called a "troop." In the heat of the day, a troop spends its time wallowing in cool mud. At night, the male babirusas use their unusual tusks to dig up the ground. When they uncover a root or a nut, they give out a happy groan. The males give the female babirusas and their babies the first chance to eat whatever is found.

Civet
(SIV-it)

Tangling with a tangalung? Mangling!

Wrangling with a delandung? Jangling!

Brawling with a binturong? Wrong!

Scrapping with sulawezi? Crazy!

Advice:

DON'T PLAY WRANGLED, TANGLED GAMES WITH CATS WHO HAVE NEW-FANGLED NAMES

Fabulous Fact

The musang is a civet that loves to drink the sap from the palm tree. The sap has a lot of alcohol in it and is made into a drink called "toddy." Sometimes musangs will drink so much sap that they get drunk and fall out of trees. That's why they're nicknamed "toddy cats."

The tangalung, delandung, binturong and sulawezi are all names for different civets that live in the jungles of Africa and Asia. And that's not all. There's also the linsang, musang, falouka, fossa and others! There are many kinds of civets but not every one has a tongue-twisting name. The civet in the illustration, for example, is simply called the "banded palm" civet . Civets are often called "cats" but they are not really cats. Look closely and you see a civet has a weasel-like face and raccoon tail.

The civet is a beautiful animal, both striped and spotted. With its long claws and sharp teeth it can be a fierce fighter, although it stays away from humans. However, the civet is not known for its looks, but its smell. This animal has a gland that makes a smelly liquid called musk, also called civet. When the civet sprays its territory with musk, other civets stay away. For more than a hundred years, the musk did not keep people away. It was the musk itself that people wanted! Why? When musk is added to perfume, it makes the perfume smell nice longer. Today people make artificial musk and it works just as well. That's good news for the lovely tangalung, delandung, binturong, and sulawezi, not to mention the linsang, musang, falouka, fossa, and other tongue-twisting civets.

Colugo
(kuh-LOO-go)

Colugo clings to tree trunks tight
Until the dark advance of night,
When shaping himself like a kite
Colugo launches into flight.

With spread-cloak skin in a single bound
He glides above the jungle ground.
From tree to tree and all around
He soars without the slightest sound.

But with the light of a brand-new day,
Just like putting a toy away,
Colugo folds up small and gray,
For on a tree trunk he must stay.

Silent, still, out of sight
Until the dark advance of night.

Fabulous Fact

Often, colugos share a tree that's particularly good for launching their flight. They line up for take-off like airplanes on a runway.

This cat-size animal lives in the rain forests of Southeast Asia. During the day, the colugo sleeps clinging to a tree trunk. You might think it looks very boring—like a burst balloon.

But wait.

At night, the colugo spreads its skin wide as a kite and takes off! It sails from tree to tree, searching for fruit, flowers and leaves. It does not fly like a bat or a bird, but sails on waves of air, like a hang glider. And like a hang glider, the colugo steers through the air with just slight movements of its body.

The colugo is at home in the rain forest but only in the trees. If a colugo is put on the ground, it can barely move, for it is unable to walk.

The colugo's teeth are unique. Each tooth is shaped like a comb. The colugo uses its teeth to comb its fur and to dig sweet sap out of tree trunks. Everything about the colugo is unusual, including the noise it makes—like a duck quacking!

Coqui
(koe-kee)

Fabulous Fact
The coqui may be small, but its song is louder than the noise of a vacuum cleaner!

When leaves in the forest drip and glisten,
When the moon is a hammock slung low,
Close your eyes, then let yourself listen.
To the music of Coqui's Night Show.

Atop a damp log, sits the tiniest frog
You can't see him in the darkening deep.
But the songs Coqui sings,
As if they had wings,
Will carry you so sweetly to sleep.

Imagine a tree frog so small, it could perch on a marble! The coqui is just that small. This tiny amphibian lives in the rainforest of Puerto Rico. Though it is small, it is powerful for the male coqui guards its territory by singing from dusk to dawn. Ko-Kee! Ko-kee!

Coquis vary in color. They are green, brown, yellow, and some are transparent! The transparent coqui takes on the color of its surroundings. This camouflage protects it from predators. Looking at a transparent coqui, you would see, as if looking through a window, all its organs, even its beating heart.

Though tiny, the coqui is a huge symbol for Puerto Ricans who love the little creature and proudly call themselves coquis. This love must flow both ways for if a coqui is ever taken from the island, it never sings again.

People say that if you fall asleep to the song of the coqui, you will have peaceful dreams. So if you're in Puerto Rico, open your window and... listen.

Dingo
(DING-goh)

Fabulous Fact
A mother dingo feeds her pups by regurgitating her latest meal into their mouths. Seconds, anyone?

Never play a game of bingo
With the sly Australian dingo
It's not that he's so fond of cheating
But rather that he's fond of eating.

His teeth are sharp as blades of steel—
A fact to know and not to feel.
He doesn't care a bit for fair play.
Should he lose, then I daresay
You might think you are the winner
When, in fact, you are the dinner.

No, never play a game of bingo
With the sly Australian dingo.
But if you choose it ...

Lose it.

The dingo may look like a dog, but don't pet it! The dingo is fearless and will attack animals much larger than itself. And yes, it is fond of eating—especially sheep. The dingo is native to Australia where the sheep farmers view the dingo as a terrible threat. No wonder. A pack of eight dingoes can kill more than 200 sheep in one night. To protect their flocks, the sheep farmers built the longest fence in the world to keep this wild dog out. The fence is 3,500 miles long!

Though the dingo looks like a dog, it is different. A dingo cannot move its ears or wag its tail. Instead of barking, the dingo lets out an eerie howl. However, if raised from birth with dogs, it will imitate a dog's bark.

Hagfish
(HAG-fish)

Fabulous Fact

Though a hagfish can eat an enormous amount of food, it can also eat very little, even nothing. A hagfish can go up to seven months without eating anything!

When a flirty hagfish
Feels like a dirty ragfish
She ties herself into a bow
And squeezes clean from head to roe.
This crazy bath appeals to eels
Who brag about how nice it feels.
Recently some children tried it.
Though these children have denied it.

You, yourself might want to try.
You might like it or ...
You might knot.

Though the hagfish is not really an eel, it is also called the slime eel, the blind eel and even—the snot eel. The hagfish has no fins or scales, no jaws, no eyes and only a tiny mouth surrounded by long whiskers. The hagfish lurks at the bottom of the ocean, buried up to its snout in mud.

To move through the mud, the hagfish's body makes slime. The slime is called mucus and it's a little like the stuff that comes out of your nose when you have a cold. The hagfish makes a lot of it. How much? A hagfish can turn a large bucket of water into slime in just minutes. The slime is useful. When a hagfish is caught, the slime allows it to slip away. When the hagfish is hungry, the slime chokes all the fish around, making them easy to catch. But often the slime becomes too much even for the hagfish itself. The slime gets up its nostril (it has just one), making it sneeze. When the hagfish gets too slimy, it ties itself into a knot which travels down its body, squeezing out the slime.

The hagfish has a strange tongue for it's completely lined with teeth! And it uses those teeth fast. In just one hour, a hagfish can eat more than its own weight of dead fish it finds on the ocean floor.

Jerboa
(jur-BO-ah)

Fabulous Fact

The jerboa has thick hair on the pads of its feet that absorb the shock of landing after its gigantic jumps.

When all the animals were in the ark
The good Lord said to Noah,
"You've got the dog; you've got the frog,
But where is that little jerboa?

"You've got the horse and the cow, of course
And snakes from python to boa.
I see a goose, and a duck on the loose
But where is that little jerboa?

"You've got the rat and sly old cat
And you've got that big bird, the moa.
There's enough in your ark for a zoological park
But where is that little jerboa?"

Then Noah searched every inch of his ark
And all the animals helped Noah
They looked in the boxes and then
Near the foxes, they found that little jerboa.

And the Lord said: "Noah, Now, you can goah."

The jerboa is so tiny you have to look hard to find it. Once you find it, you have to look quickly. The jerboa can jump faster than you can run. Some jerboas, no bigger than your fist, can jump 12 feet in one flying leap. Using its tufted tail for steering, the jerboa can even change course mid-flight! This Olympic gymnastic skill helps the jerboa dodge danger instantly. It also helps when it hunts for insects at night.

The jerboa lives in the deserts of North Africa and Central Asia. Like many rodents, it lives on seeds, grasses and insects. During the hot day, it stays in its underground hole which it plugs up with earth to keep in the moisture. Here, the jerboa sleeps standing up and rolled forward into a ball. It gets pretty cramped like this, so when it wakes up the first thing the jerboa does is leave the hole, stretch, and roll around in the sand. Ahhhhh.

Kinkajou
(KING-kuh-joo)

A kinkajou doesn't think of you
As she goes about her day.
You needn't exist
For you're not even missed,
Her mind is so far away.

It might just appall you
That she doesn't call you
Let alone send you
Hugs or money.

But you won't take it so hard
That you don't get a card
When you learn that her mind
Is on
Honey.

Fabulous Fact

The kinkajou makes a variety of noises. It can chirp and whistle like a bird, yelp like a dog, huff, shriek and even whisper.

The kinkajou is often called a "honey bear." It is not a bear but it does have strong claws, round ears and thick fur, and like a bear, it loves honey. The kinkajou always looks like it is having fun. It lives in the treetops of the rainforests of Central and South America and jumps noisily from tree to tree. It also sucks nectar out of flowers and feasts on bugs, mice and birds.

The kinkajou hunts at night, and has excellent vision. If a light shines onto its gigantic eyes, they will seem to glow and can be seen from far away. During the day, the kinkajou sleeps inside a hollow tree. Male kinkajous like to hang from their long tails upside down and playfully box one another in the head. Kinkajous have feet that can turn completely backwards so they can run fast in different directions.

Kinkajous have a nature just as sweet as the honey they eat. When they eat honey from a beehive, sometimes the honey drips all over its face and fur and they get all sticky. But kinkajous are as sweet as the honey for they spend time grooming each other, combing each other's fur with their claws and licking off that messy honey.

Loris
(LAW-ris)

Fabulous Fact
The loris is named for its funny face. The word "loris" comes from the Dutch word for clown.

There's a loris in our chorus
Who's truly roly-poly,
And that loris in our chorus
Is singing much too slowly.

We've begged him to sing quicker,
To liven up his pace,
But all he does is bicker,
Saying, "Singing's not a race."

There's a loris in our chorus
Who is really fat and furry.
And that loris in our chorus
Is impossible to hurry!

This animal really sings and does everything slowly. In fact the full name for some species of loris is "slow loris." Native to the jungles of Southeast Asia, the loris likes to sing to other lorises in a high-pitched voice. But if startled, the loris will open its mouth wide and let out a scary, buzzing sound.

It moves hand over hand slowly through the tops of the trees—so slowly that the leaves do not even move as it passes by.

During the day, the loris tucks its head and arms between its legs and sleeps holding on to a branch with a powerful grip. It looks like a big ball of fur. At night, the loris hunts insects, lizards and bird eggs. When the loris is thirsty, it simply touches a wet leaf then sucks the water from its fingers. Easy.

Manatee
(MAN-uh-tee)

Should you spot a manatee
Don't think you've lost your sanity.
The odds of seeing one are rare,
But if you do, it's really there.
The manatee is just as real
As a turtle, fish, or seal.
So move in for a closer look
Or learn about it from a book.
Then should you spot the sleek dugong
You know you will not get it wrong,
And mistake a manatee for his cousin.
Yes, even if you spot a dozen
You'll know the fact that never fails:

ONLY MANATEES HAVE SPOON-SHAPED TAILS.

Fabulous Fact

Manatees like to play "follow the leader." They sometimes move in a single file and coordinate their movements such as breathing, diving and changing direction like synchronized swimmers!

Manatees and dugongs are large marine mammals, more related to elephants than to whales or dolphins. They are as big as cows and like cows, they travel in herds, produce milk and graze on grass—sea grass that grows underwater. The manatee swims along the coast of Florida, South America and Africa. It is gentle and likes to play. It's fun to watch a manatee body surf and do barrel rolls!

The dugong is a close relative of the manatee, living in the coastal waters of Australia.

Can you tell them apart? Of course you can! The manatee has a rounded tail like a beaver's. The dugong's tail is split like a whale's or like the mythical mermaid's. In fact, because dugongs are sleek and graceful, some early sailors thought dugongs were mermaids.

Manatees and dugongs belong to the species, sirenia. Because they are mammals, they need to come up often for air, but when they are excited, they dive deep and let out a loud whistle! And this is how we got the word "siren."

Matamata
(MA-ta-MA-ta)

Fabulous Fact

The matamata has frills on its neck. The frills detect even slight movements of water. In this way the frills let the matamata know there's a fish nearby so it can get ready to attack.

Matamata waiting all alone,
Looking like a leafy stone.
Along comes a fish and bites his back
Thinking leaves are a tasty snack.

**ATTACK!
THE SNACK BITES BACK!**

That hapless fish is swallowed quick!
And this was matamata's trick:
Making that hungry, hasty fish
Think matamata was the tasty dish.

The matamata is a very tricky turtle. Its shell is made up of many skin flaps shaped like leaves and covered with algae. These flaps sway and drift with the water currents. The matamata looks as if it is a plant of tasty green leaves. In South America, at the bottom of the Amazon River, the matamata sits without moving until a fish comes along and tries to nibble on a leaf. With lightning speed, the matamata stretches its long neck and swallows the fish whole.

Matamata has other ways of catching fish. This turtle walks along the river, herding fish as it goes. The matamata corners them against a rock then sucks them up with its big mouth— as swiftly as a vacuum cleaner.

Unlike other turtles, matamatas never bask in the sun and they are poor swimmers. Their breathing is different too. They breathe by extending their neck so that their long snout sticks up above the water, making them look as if they are snorkeling.

Okapi
(oh-KAH-pee)

Authentic
Beautiful
Curious
Different
Extraordinary
First
Genuine
Handsome
Individual
Jungle-dwelling
Kind
Lone
Magnificent
Novel
Original

Particular
Quirky
Rare
Special
Terrific
Unique
Vital
Weird
Xceptional
Yellow-eared
Zebra-striped

Okapi
No Copy.

Fabulous Fact

If a giraffe invited all its relatives to its birthday party, the okapi would be the only guest.

The okapi is really one of a kind. What other animal do you know that has purplish fur, a striped behind, and a tongue long enough to clean its ears? The okapi is related to the giraffe and looks like a cross between a zebra and a horse. It is not as tall as a giraffe: it stands about as high as a pony.

The okapi lives in only one place in the world: in the dark and damp Ituri rainforest, located in the Democratic Republic of the Congo. It eats the lower leaves of the trees.

The okapi is a shy, gentle animal. It moves about alone, silently blending into the deep shadows of the forest. In this quiet, secretive way it keeps out of sight of leopards. In fact, the okapi has survived for centuries because it is so hard to see. The colors of the okapi are the same colors and patterns of the dark, shadowed forest in which it lives. You could be standing really close to an okapi and not even see it.

The okapi was discovered in 1901. It was the last mammal to be discovered by scientists in the 20th century. In the thick forest, the okapi is so well hidden that we hardly know more about it today than we did in 1901. Wouldn't you like to know more?

Tamandua
(ta-MAN-dyo-uh)

I've got ants on my fingers,
Got termites on my tongue,
But I've never been bit,
I've never been stung!

Why don't you come and try it?
Lots of crawlies for your lunch.
It's a really tasty diet,
Eating bugs by the bunch!

And... then... you'll sing...

I've got ants on my fingers,
Got termites on my tongue,
But I've never been bit,
I've never been stung!

Why don't you come and try it?
Lots of crawlies for your lunch.
It's a really tasty diet,
Eating bugs by the bunch!

Fabulous Fact

Tamanduas never destroy a whole ant or termite nest. They eat only a portion of the colony, then move on to the next one. By preserving the colonies, they ensure their future food.

How would you like to be called "stinker of the forest"? No? Well, that's the name that the local people in the Amazon rain forest give to the tamandua. When a tamandua feels threatened by another animal, its glands produce a nasty smell. It's the kind of smell that would make you run and leave it alone.

The tamandua is a type of anteater that lives in Central and South America. Its nose is long and so is its powerful tail by which it hangs from a tree branch. But its mouth is as tiny as the eraser on your pencil! The tamandua doesn't need a big mouth because what it eats is small: termites, grubs, bees, and ants. The tamandua's mouth may be small but its saliva is super-sticky. It can drop its super-long tongue 16 inches down a termite hole and reel it up with hundreds of termites stuck to it. Tamanduas also lick their paws to make them sticky so they can easily pick up ants and just lick them off their fingers. Yum.

Tasmanian Devil
(taz-MEY-nee-un)

Those folks who named me
"Devil"
Did not use their brains!
I'm really not as devilish
As everybody claims.
This bad name
Appalls me!
It absolutely galls me!

MAKES ME WANT TO BITE YOU!
FEROCIOUSLY FIGHT YOU!
TO MUNCH AND CRUNCH!
AND EAT YOU UP FOR LUNCH!

So I'm sure you won't mind
Since I'm really so kind,
Renaming me,
and claiming me
TASMANIAN ANGEL.

Fabulous Fact

The Tasmanian Devil prefers to eat already dead animals. Because it eats the entire animal, the Devil helps to prevent the spread of disease.

Have you seen Taz, the Tasmanian Devil in a Bugs Bunny cartoon? If so, you haven't seen the Tasmanian Devil at all. The real Tasmanian Devil looks nothing like the cartoon character. It looks like a cross between a dog and a cat. It also looks scarier because it is scarier. This animal is only the size of a small dog but is as fierce as a tiger.

The Tasmanian Devil lives on the Australian island of Tasmania. With its huge, powerful jaws it will eat anything. It devours both live and dead animals of any kind, eating all bones, fur and feathers. A Tasmanian Devil will even eat another Tasmanian Devil!

The Devil's black fur is a great camouflage when it hunts for food at night. When threatened, it gives off a really bad smell and becomes vicious. And to top it off, the animal opens its enormous mouth and sends out a terrifying sound. It starts like a loud whistle and ends in a spine-chilling screech and...what? You're going back to the cartoon?

Wait—There's more!

You've met strange animals from cover to cover.

Now, how many more can you discover?

Here is a nice alphabetical list

Of other rare animals not to be missed!

Aye Aye	Numbat
Bilby	Oryx
Capybara	Pichiciego
Duiker	Quagga
Eland	Ratel
Falanaka	Saiga
Guanaco	Tamarin
Hutia	Unau
Indri	Vicuna
Jutia	Wombat
Kowari	Xenopus
Langur	Yapok
Muntjac	Zoril

There are so many more little-known animals. In fact, new ones are being discovered all the time. Scientists estimate that many thousands of species have yet to be identified—especially ones living in the oceans. Pick an animal, find out about it, and tell your friends about it.

Sounds Like

(a phonics activity)

Suggestions for teachers: write the names of the animals on the board. As you read aloud each name, point out phonics patterns, such as the two different ways the letter "c" is pronounced in colugo and in civet, and the two ways the letter "a" is pronounced in hagfish and okapi. Then have children take turns reading the animal names to a partner.

What's In a Name?

Using the Okapi poem as a model, pick a name of any animal and write its attributes using the letters that make up that animal's name. For example: Jerboa

Jumping
Energetic
Rolling
Bouncy
Olympic skill
African

Rhyme Twins

(A fluency and phonics exercise)

Pick a poem and read it aloud to a partner. Have them listen for "rhyme twins"—two (or more) words that rhyme with each other. Then write them down. It's especially fun when words can be spelled very differently yet still rhyme, such as "tongue" and "stung." Examples can be found throughout the book. Then create a simple two-line poem about a different animal, especially an animal that lives near where you live, using the same rhyming words.

Dingoes and Dogs

(A comprehension and graphic organizing exercise)

Suggestion for teachers: have readers form pairs. Assign two animals to each pair, choosing one animal from the book plus one locally familiar animal. Ask partners to make a list of how their animals are the same and how they are different. Have them use their lists to create a Venn diagram, which can be posted on a bulletin board.

Ghostwriters

(A comprehension exercise)

Choose an animal and then write a postcard that that animal might send to your class. Even better, use a 3x5 card to create a real postcard with a photo or drawing on one side and writing on the other—combining writing and art, just as this book does. Here are some ideas:

What would the animal say it was doing?

What would make a good day for the animal?

A bad day?

What would the animal's return address be?

How would the animal describe the food where it lives?

The scenery?

The other animals?

The sounds it hears?

Fact or Fancy?

(A comprehension and graphic organizing exercise)

Suggestion for teachers: on a chalkboard or a piece of paper make a table with two columns, one titled "fact" (or "real") and one titled "fancy" (or "make believe," or "fiction"). Ask the children to identify which things about an animal are real and which things are fancy, and list in the appropriate column. What clues in the book help them tell the difference? This is especially good as a small-group activity in which each group gets an animal. Each group can conclude by sharing their most "unusual fact" and most "outrageous fancy" with the whole class.

Word Wall

(a vocabulary and comprehension activity)

Suggestion for teachers: create a Word Wall by posting the names of all of the curious creatures on a wall or bulletin board. Underneath each name, post a 3x5 card for each new vocabulary word found in the poem or passage. Have the vocabulary word written on the front of the card and the definition written on the back. Ask children to read about an animal and use the context to write down a possible definition for each new vocabulary word. When finished, have them look at the back of the card to read the correct definition. Then have them read the poem and passage again.

Hidden Pictures – Accept the Challenge!

There's a hidden picture in every main illustration. Can you find it? The picture refers to something mentioned in the poem or in the text.

Babirusa:	Boxing glove
Civet:	Scrabble pieces spelling out BINTURONG
Colugo:	Airplane on a runway
Coqui:	A heart
Dingo:	Dog bowl with the name Dingo on it
Hagfish:	Boy Scout Merit Badge for knots
Jerboa:	Olympic medal for the high jump
Kinkajou:	Honey pot
Loris:	Clown face
Manatee:	Mermaid
Matamata:	Neon sign that says "Fast Food"
Okapi:	Birthday party hat
Tamandua:	Pencil
Tasmanian Devil:	Whistle

AUTHOR

Maxine Rose Schur is an award-winning travel essayist and the author of critically-acclaimed books for children including novels, biography, and picture books. Maxine lives in the San Francisco Bay Area. To learn more about her books, writing classes and speaking engagements, go to:

www.maxineroseschur.com.

ILLUSTRATOR

Michael S. Maydak is passionate about nature, especially the riparian environments that he loves so much as a fly fisherman. Mike is an art graduate of San Jose University and has been a professional artist since 1976. Mike works out of his studio at his home in Cool, California.

Want more insightful, empowering, fun children's books?

For more books parents can trust and kids will love, visit us at

www.lawleypublishing.com

For updates and info on New Releases follow us at

lawleypublishing

@kidsbookswithheart

www.ingramcontent.com/pod-product-compliance
Lightning Source LLC
Chambersburg PA
CBRC100225100526
44592CB00007B/92